THE BARON

The Dog Who Trained Me

by Allen & Rufus Plone

THE BARON
The Dog Who Trained Me

©2021 by Allen Plone

All rights exclusively reserved. No part of this book may be reproduced or translated into any language or utilized in any form or by any means, electronic or mechanical, including photocopying, recording or by any information storage and retrieval system, without permission in writing from the publisher.

Words & Photography by Allen Plone
with help from Rufus, aka The Baron

Interior and Cover design by Mark E. Anderson

AquaZebra.com

Published by Snow Lion Publishing
Los Angeles, CA

ISBN: 978-1-954604-03-2

Library of Congress Control Number: 2021909141

First Edition
First Printing, April 2021

Printed in the United States of America

DEDICATION

To all the wonderful animal companions who share our life and to Carol, my love and inspiration always.

I

This is a story about a dog and his human companion—me. He came to us from a rescue group called Bichon and Buddies. He's a buddy, not a bichon. This, according to his DNA, is his genetic makeup: 37.5% miniature poodle, 12.5% Pomeranian, 12.5% Maltese, 12.5% Shih Tzu, the rest pure mutt. He came with a name—Rufus. It didn't take long before we realized he needed an honorific title, one that represented his high status and dignified behavior. He became The Baron. Shortened from his full title, Baron Rufulstein Von Pfeffernusse. It has become his *nom de plume.*

Rufus was twice abandoned by families he thought were his home forever. One of the great mysteries for me, after he and I became best friends, was why he was given up by these people. Their loss was surely our gain. Yes, Rufus has his little quirks; he doesn't like mail people, FedEx drivers, UPS deliveries, gardeners with tools in the hands. He barks and barks, sounding like the most vicious guard dog this side of a junk yard. And he'll snap when he feels cornered or afraid. But most of the time, and always with us, he is the most gentle and loving companion a person can have.

He sang us a song on the first day he came home.

Just Rufus

I'm just Rufus
and I do my best
I make mistakes,
that's true
But doesn't everyone,
even you?
I try to love you
best I can
but you just quit
and sent me packin'
(chorus)
I never knew why
they never said goodbye
Somethin' that I did or said?
I'm gettin' tired of the life I led.

Clearly, he didn't want his heart broken as it had twice before.

Like so many other times during our life together, his songs broke my heart, made me hug him tighter, somewhat against his will, gave him several extra belly rubs and a promise that this time, this place would be different. He was home for good.

Notice the eyes. It was the soulful nature of his eyes and his noble bearing that first drew me to him. Can you imagine anyone abandoning this guy?

II

Rufus came to us—my partner and wife, Carol, and myself—after forty-plus years of being cat people. He was my first dog. Ever. I had much to learn about dogs; how they differed from cats, for instance. Not just the obvious, or the clichés about how cats are aloof. Our cats were great companions, anything but aloof. Most always choosing to be with us, wanting attention and closeness just, as I had imagined, like a dog. Perhaps the biggest adaptation for us was to understand that dogs require more of your time. You can't leave a dog home alone for the weekend unless you want your home turned into a cesspool. Dogs understand, or at least respond to, more words than cats. I've read that the average dog knows and responds to over three hundred words.

Though I had fantasies about having a dog companion, with my lifestyle, lots of traveling, little time to devote to anything but Carol, our daughter and my work, I chose, always, to stay with cats.

The Baron Sings the Stones

when I dreamed dog
he sat beside me
Saluki blond hair
breeze-blown
in our convertible
top down best pal
cruising

this white curly head
sleeping on the sedan floor
avoiding the wind
the antonym
of my imagination

the Baron
came to me
not from a dream
but in the reality of abandonment
knowing in his wisdom
we belonged to each other

proving Jagger's wisdom
you can't always get what you want
but
you get what you need

III

Let's talk cats to begin. My first cat, **Bourgeois** (so named because she and I lived in a condominium in Aptos, CA), was a sleek black beauty. She had amazing hunting skills, a trait—admittedly—I found a bit disturbing when she'd leave me a lizard's tail or feet and feathers from a bird she caught. But I loved her and accepted our differences. Bourg was an Amazon warrior, great hunter and loyal friend. She was that rare cat that liked taking walks with me. She and I would take the backwoods trail to the beach. That's as far as she'd go. No beach. She didn't like the sand and didn't like the wide-open spaces. If I walked farther on, she'd sit and wait for me to return. She and I were buddies for six years before she decided she wanted to live on a farm and catch mice for a living. Reluctantly, I let her go seek the life her heart told her to live.

It wasn't long after she left us, that I knew I wanted someone to fill the space she left in my heart.

Kishka

Our second cat (by this time it wasn't me, it was us, as Carol joined the pack and quickly became the Alpha female) came to share our home as a stray who truly adopted us. It happened this way.

It was a dark and stormy night. Truly. Carol and I were sitting at our kitchen table; she with coffee, I with a cup of tea. We had been discussing what kind of cat we should adopt. I wanted an Abyssinian. I loved their silly personalities and equally beautiful faces. Carol was okay with any cat.

We heard a knock at the back door. Wait! No one came calling at our back door. Besides, the San Francisco rain was unforgiving. We looked at each other. Another knock. Summoning up all my courage, I went to the door and opened it. In strolled this lovely cat—a young one we could tell—completely dry, despite the weather. She meowed, looked up at me and said, "Pay the cabbie. I'm your cat."

And so she became ours. We called her Kishka, a Yiddish term for cow's intestines, because she was so gutsy. For several days Kishka was the sweetest, most friendly cat ever. We put up posters around the neighborhood with her picture on them. We advertised in the paper. No takers. She was truly a stray.

After a week, we agreed that she was officially ours. Once she heard that, she decided to show her true personality. Kishka was the smartest, most devious and devilish cat ever. She attacked dogs, scratching their noses, making most of them run off whimpering. If you annoyed her, in any way, she'd stalk off, then sometime later when you least expected it, she come strolling back into the room, mosey over to where you were, and deliver a swipe at whatever spot had the most of your skin showing. Then she'd stare at you and walk off again. Most of our friends were terrified of her, having felt her claws and teeth on too many occasions. She left me scarred, since one of her favorite tricks was to roll over onto her back, expose her tummy and seemingly invite you to give it a few good rubs. As soon as she knew she had you, your hand on her belly, all four claws would clamp down, followed by a less-than-gentle bite. Then she'd leave—letting you nurse your wounds—and strut off snickering. Interestingly, she never bit or scratched Carol. Kishka was, like Carol, a deeply felt feminist.

We had the joy and pain that Kishka brought for seventeen years, bringing an end to her time, and to the seizures she developed, with a final visit to the vet. We cried for several days and wondered if we'd ever get over her loss.

But we gave in. We decided to foster rescue cats. Mitzie, plus four newly born kittens, eyes not yet opened, were our first experiment with fostering. Mitzie, a scrawny alley cat, came with four ten-day-old kittens. When the kittens were about six weeks old, Mitzie died of what we discovered was a congenital heart disease. We hand-fed the kittens, raised them until they were weaned then decided to keep two, Pandora and Catcher. We found a good home for the other two with a close friend of ours, Naomi.

Catcher quickly became Carol's cat. He loved her. Pandy was all mine. She was the one who proved to be the hardest act to follow.

Pandora

Pandy and I bonded deeply. We grew to have what must be called, even if you're a doubter, a psychic connection. No matter where she was or what she was doing, all I had to do was think about her and she'd come to be with me. Like her namesake, she was a one-cat wrecking machine. Pandy didn't like to jump, preferring to claw her way up things: clothes in closets, paper lampshades, sofas, chairs, an antique kimono displayed on our wall. Any hanging object that looked inviting. We estimated that over her life span she destroyed about fifteen thousand dollars' worth of stuff. I guess you could say we were overindulgent.

Pandy lived only to the age of fourteen. She contracted lymphoma. We made the mistake of trying to keep her alive using extraordinary measures: chemo, hydration, and constant vet visits. She hated it all. She was in pain, dis-oriented from the chemo and upset by the hydration needles. She died six weeks after the diagnosis, having dropped from a hearty eleven-pound cat to just over five pounds.

Catcher

Catcher, just eleven months later, developed the same disease. We learned the lesson Pandora had taught us: When a companion knows or feels it's their time to go, if you love them, you will let them go with grace and without pain. I talked to Catcher, told him I didn't want him to suffer, I didn't particularly want to take him to the vet to be euthanized. I asked him, if he could, please, when it's time, die peacefully at home, accompanied in his final journey by myself and Carol.

It was a terrible day. A Thursday. Catcher was dying. As I sat with him, held him and loved him, I thought about his life and times. The infinite moments we had shared over the last nearly-fifteen years. I reflected not only upon the joy he and his sister, Pandora, had brought us, but upon the other cats who had shared my life. Yes, I was a confirmed cat person.

I knew that this was his last day. Now too weak to jump up on the sofa or, for that matter, walk too much. I carried him to wherever I sat or worked. At that moment, he was on my desk, next to my keyboard. As had his sister, he had dropped from his normal twelve pounds to about six. He looked like a scrawny scruff ball. As do cats in their last days, he had stopped grooming himself. He let out a soft sound, somewhere between a purr and a meow. I looked at him. He was telling me it was time.

I called Carol at her work; after all, Catcher was her cat. I told her to come home as soon as possible. Catcher was near the end. I lifted him up, carried him to the sofa, sat down, and put him on my lap. He lay there, quiet, with slightly labored breathing. About fifteen minutes later, Carol came home. She sat down next to me on the couch. Catcher looked up at her, reached out his paw and laid it on her hand. And died.

We wrapped his sadly thin body in his favorite blanket, placed him in the car, ready to take him for his last ride to the vet. In a fit of anger and grief at his dying, I gathered every toy, every cat bowl, litter box, cans, bags of food and threw them into the back of the car. We drove to the vet, where we donated all the stuff and surrendered him, for the last time, into her care. His paw print, in a baked clay heart sits next to my desk.

On our drive back home Carol and I swore that Catcher was the last animal companion we'd ever have. The pain of losing the two best cats that ever lived was too great and, at that moment, overwhelmed any of the joy they had brought us.

Catcher catching sunshine in our house.

IV

Three months since Catcher died, I still hadn't gotten over his death, and truth be told, not Pandora's either. My insistence that I never wanted to have another companion animal grew stronger, I thought, feeling I couldn't and didn't want to go through another loss. Grief haunts me, a family ghost that follows too closely behind.

Carol is the more practical. She, in many ways, has learned to accept the world as it comes to her. She is my rock and guide. Too many times in my life, when I went off on a tangent, following some scheme to folly, she's the shore to which I swim for safety. In many ways, she's the wiser of we two. In her gentle way, she helped me get over my anger and grief.

Carol has always been an ardent visitor of dog rescue websites. Even as cat people, we loved dogs. Dogs loved Carol. We'd meet them and they'd ignore me and fawn all over her. Cats, however, seemed to take to me; I talked to them and they usually talked back. I had no idea what I was saying, just trying to imitate the sounds I heard them make, but they seemed to know what I meant and that was enough. Animals speak. It's up to we humans to learn how to listen.

Maira Kalman said it best in her great book, *Beloved Dog*. She's a wonderful, magical illustrator and writer. This to her loved dog, Pete, after he died:

> During our years together, I often asked Pete to say one word to me. Just one word. It is like asking to hear one word from a loved one who has died. Give me a sign you have not really left me. It is not going to happen. But it does not stop you from wishing and hoping for a miracle. So I would beg Pete to say one word. He never did. But of course, he spoke volumes.

A few months passed. The loss weighed on us. But, to our fortune, we had each other to love, together remember the joy of our cat partners, to laugh at our own follies allowing them to be destroyers of property, but never of love. We loved all animals. To the extent, that I have been a vegan for 26 years. Though we, neither of us, wanted to share our lives with them, our fascination with dogs went so far that we had bought a home across from a dog park just so we could watch and sometimes play with them without disturbing our cats. We believed we had the best of it; we could watch, and occasionally visit, other people's dogs without the annoyance of walking them, grooming them or having to make our plans around their needs.

One afternoon, Carol emailed me from her work. One of the sites she visited on a regular basis, Bichons and Buddies, had this adorable fluff ball who was described as the perfect dog. I went online and saw the bichon mix she mentioned. He was cute, for sure. But a bit above his picture I noticed another dog. This dog had the most soulful eyes and doleful look I had seen since the dog who's so worried about losing his bone on the Traveler's Insurance commercial.

His name, I read, was Rufus. His picture really got to me. That evening Carol and I talked about dogs and companion animals in general and decided that cute as they were, we didn't want to take on the responsibility. And I, especially, didn't want to suffer through another loss.

Over the next two weeks or so, I visited the Bichon and Buddies website with some regularity. Each time Rufus' sad look captured me. I noticed that Bichon and Buddies was having an adoption event. Carol and I talked about going; but only to look, certainly not to adopt. I just wanted to meet that sad little doggie, Rufus. Carol was skeptical. Her motto has always been if you don't want to buy anything don't go to a store.

Saturday it was rainy, unusual for Los Angeles. The scheduled Bichon and Buddies event was cancelled as an outdoor one and moved inside to the Robertson Avenue home, where many of their dogs were boarded. Carol and I showed up at about one-thirty. Bichon and Buddies was founded by Jeanine Curcione. She has been

> ...dedicated to the rescue of homeless and unwanted Bichons, Bichon-mixes, and other small dog breeds since 2004, making certain that they are placed in a home that provides them with the love and care they deserve.

We were greeted at the door by one of the volunteers. Her dog tag told us that her name was Leslie. We told Leslie we had come to see Rufus and one other dog (I think his name was Winston). Several other people—a family of four, a young couple with one child—were also waiting to meet some new furry friends. Suddenly there was a rush of white as four or five dogs came barreling out of the back into the visiting room. Leslie brought us Winston. I asked her if she had brought Rufus. "No," she said. "Rufus wasn't ready to come out."

Carol and I took Winston, a lovely little Bichon mix, out for a walk. He was a good, energetic dog, well-behaved and gentle. We went around the block a couple of times, then sat on some stairs. He came and sat next to Carol. He was a great dog, for sure. We took him back to the mass of fur that was the visiting room and handed him back to Leslie. "Can we see Rufus?" I asked.

We waited for several minutes, watching dogs and people find one another. After about ten minutes, Leslie reappeared with this beautiful dog; the one with the soulful look that, by this time, I recognized. Rufus had finally made his appearance. He looked as sad as he did in his photos. Leslie handed us the leash and we headed for the door. Rufus reluctantly followed. We barely got him outside. He didn't want to take a walk. I picked him up, surprised at his heft, and carried him across the street to a little patch of grass. Carol and I sat next to him. Leslie was with us, concerned that Rufus wasn't being cooperative and wasn't showing well. Rufus sat down. And stayed that way. Carol and I looked at him, petted him, scratched him. He wasn't indifferent, just, well, wary.

Leslie picked Rufus up and carried him back to the visiting room. Carol and I sat on the floor. She put Rufus down to mingle with the other dogs. Rufus moved off as far away from the pack as possible and sat. The other dogs jumped on us, gave us kisses, played with us. Rufus sat. Time passed. We were ready to leave, and then, quite suddenly, on my left, close by, there sat Rufus. He walked over to Carol—whose depth of caring and love is easily recognized by animals—and nuzzled her hand. She gave him good scratches behind the ears and on his belly. He then circled over to where I was sitting, came close and leaned on me. I scratched his soft ears. Both of us had started to cry. Jeanine watched. Rufus was now unwilling to leave us; and that was fine. "You can foster him, you know, try him out. See if it works for you guys." Jeanine said.

Carol looked at me: "He needs us."

Against all our protestations of never having another companion, Rufus came home with us. Foster? Not a chance. Once he walked into our lives it was certain he'd never walk out.

I realize, now, that Rufus had taught me my first life lesson: sometimes it isn't about what's best for you or what you might want or need; it's about hearing the voice and the needs of another being and reaching out to fulfill that need they have so generously shared with you. It's about learning to listen to the way others communicate, not insist that they speak your language. It's about listening, both to your own heart and to others. The greater good, Rufus showed me, is to respond to the greater need.

The Baron Upon His Throne

Old Baron Von Pfeffernusse sits observing the world.
From his throne, he judges whether all is good or not so.

With half-open eyes, he studies each being who passes.
In a flash he decides if it's good to eat or worth chasing.

If it rains, he thinks, I will not take my daily walk.
Instead, I will nap for an additional hour.

So many choices a Baron must make
comes with the title given.
Royal as I am, I must do no less for the world.

Head high, chest out, he displays his most masterly mien.
He leaves no doubt who the lord of the manor might be.

Tired of sharing his nobility, he slowly lowers his lids.
Yawning, showing his canines, with one tail wag,
he dismisses all.

V

See how his nose isn't all black? That's depigmentation. It looked to me like a pfeffernusse cookie. Those not familiar with German, *pfeffernusse* translates as "pepper nose."

THE BARON

Pfeffernusse is a famous tiny spice cookie, popular as a holiday treat in Germany, Denmark, and The Netherlands, as well as among ethnic Mennonites in North America. Great for people. Not so much for dogs.

Recipe for Pfeffernusse Cookies

Picture and recipe courtesy of https://farmtojar.com/pfeffernusse-for-college-care-packages/

Ingredients:
1/2 cup molasses
1/4 cup honey
1/2 cup butter
2 eggs slightly beaten
2 tsp anise extract
4 cups all-purpose flour
3/4 cups white sugar
1/2 cup brown sugar
1 1/2 tsp ground cardamom grind it fresh if possible
1 tsp freshly ground nutmeg
1 tsp ground cloves freshly ground if possible
1 tsp ground ginger
2 tsp ground cinnamon
1 1/2 tsp baking soda
1 tsp freshly ground black pepper can use 2 tsp white pepper for color
1/2 tsp salt
1 cup powdered sugar for dusting

Directions:

In a medium saucepan over medium heat, combine molasses, honey, and butter and cook, stirring frequently. Cook until creamy and thoroughly mixed together. Remove from heat and allow to cool. When mixture is cool, stir in the eggs and the anise extract.

In a large bowl, whisk together the dry ingredients, including the flour, sugars, and spices (but not the powdered sugar). Add the molasses mixture and stir together thoroughly. Refrigerate for 2 hours or overnight.

Preheat oven to 325° F. Let the dough thaw slightly so it is pliable enough to roll into balls. Roll into small balls, about 1-1/4" in size. Place on baking sheet, about 1" apart (they don't spread much but they do get a little bigger when baked).

Bake for 10-12 minutes, they should be slightly brown on the bottom. Cool a minute on the sheet and then transfer cookies to wire rack to cool completely. Use a sifter to dust cookies with powdered sugar.

I expect to pass through the world but once.

Any good, therefore, that I can do or any kindness to any creature, let me do it now. Let me not defer it.

—Quaker Saying

VI

Having a new roommate requires adjustments in lifestyle. An example: If you once ran around your house naked, you now need to put something on before you get a cup of coffee and check your messages. Rufus didn't mind us running around the house naked or our checking our messages, but he did radically alter our schedules.

Dogs need walks. No litter boxes. Plus and minus to that one. Dogs like schedules; walked the same time, fed the same time. I discovered that dogs developed routines and wanted to be able to depend on their needs being met when and as expected. I also quickly found out the dogs are more expensive than cats. More vet visits, more food, more grooming. More of everything that costs money. This was the least of the problems, though, in getting used to having Rufus as our roommate.

Our first chore, an obvious one, was to find all of life's necessities for him; food he liked (when he first came to us he was a fussy eater), toys, treats, leash, harness, tags that identified him as belonging in our house and, of course, a comfortable bed.

The morning following his joining us, we went to Centinela Pet to find what he needed. Reluctantly (which, as we found out, was how Rufus approached any hint of a walk), he came into the store with us.

He stopped at the door, sniffed, lifted his leg and peed. Carol was embarrassed. I laughed and assured her, given the state of the door post, that Rufus wasn't the first dog to mark that particular spot.

A display of dog beds sat about twenty feet from the door. Rufus went right for it, jumped into the one designed for a small horse, and settled down. He wasn't going to move from that bed. Okay, we thought, he picked a nice bed.

Not understanding dog-speak yet, we encouraged him to get up from his choice and look around a little more to see if there was one that he liked better. We had to lift him out of the bed to get him going; he had determined he was quite comfortable and saw no reason to move. We coaxed him along until we found the aisle where the beds lived. I pulled out the medium-size version of the one he preferred. He jumped in and again settled down.

I went to another bed I thought he might like and laid it out on the floor. Rufus roused himself, got out of his now-favorite bed, walked slowly over to the one I'd found for him, lifted his leg and peed on it, strolled back to the bed he had chosen and jumped back in. I thought it was great. Carol not so much. Rufus had just taught me a second lesson in communicating with him.

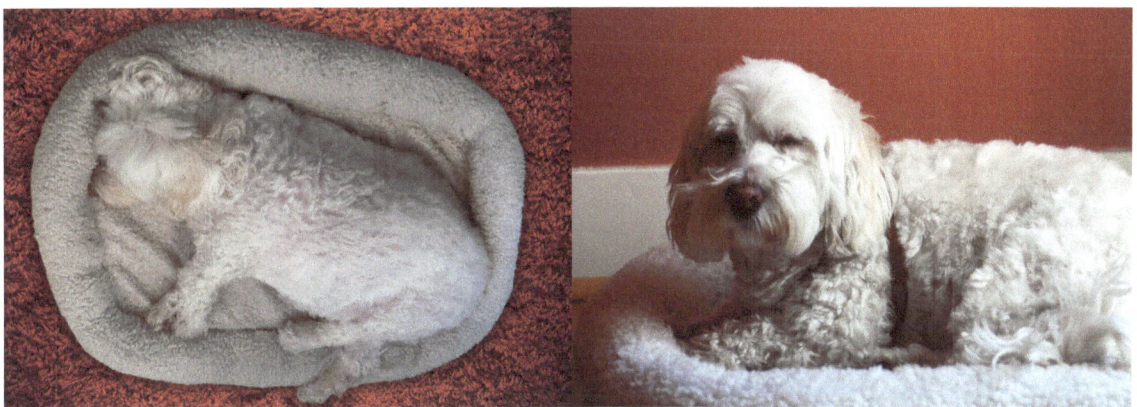

Rufus in his bed, the one he chose.

Rufus loves his bed. He also loves sleeping with us on our bed, often burrowing under the covers or pushing pillows aside to mold himself a nest. Each day that passed Rufus seemed a little more comfortable and a little less depressed. We knew he was a good dog, even though we were novices at having a canine companion, but he often surprised us with so many non-dog-like behaviors he showed. Little things, like not devouring his food as soon as it hit his new bowl, or not wanting to play in the dog park or take walks. He was reluctant to leave the house. He shied away from his leash and harness.

Really? You want me to wear a harness? Ain't happenin'...

When we brought out his leash, he'd begin to shiver. Carol thought that it very clearly indicated that he was punished by being hit with his leash in the past. I hid the leash in my pocket and made certain that it never dangled in a threatening way. Carol began to take the leash and lay it near him, then offer a treat. We felt great when, after several months, he stopped fearing the leash. We understood: He was beginning to trust us.

Rufus seemed to have a bladder the size of an elephant's, sometimes not peeing for more than twelve hours. This walk-thing confused us. So many years of being with cats seemed poor training for having a dog companion. But at this stage of our relationship, Rufus wasn't ready or willing to let go of his secrets and tell us what was going on and what he really wanted, even if he was quick to let us know what he didn't want. Once, when Carol tried to get him out from under the covers (he usually squirmed to the middle, where he was hardest to get to), he gave her a warning growl and bared teeth. Wasn't hard to figure out that bit of communication.

The Baron Quotes Walpole

The Baron asleep in his den
dark cool quiet
undisturbed by nature or its call

hears me grab his leash
Pfeffernusse says I
it's time for your walk
marked by the clock

not by need
on his part at least
time no factor for him
he does not stir
nor deign to lift his head

only grumbles his *ruff*
what's that you say
ever ready to listen
to the Baron's demands

I'm certain I understand
his varying barks
haven't you yet learned
as the old saying goes

let sleeping dogs lie

The Baron Orders Room Service

only *haute cuisine* suits
venison if you please
served upon finest plates
set neatly at his feet

he has his place at table
The Baron does most sure
at the head he sits serene
barking for seconds please

manners set aside
he needs no knife or fork
a set of canines does fine
& a tongue to lap the plate

he sits lordly calls for treats
to move from my plate to his
even if he hates to say so
it's my help he surely needs

well after all   he ruffs
if I had opposing thumbs
I wouldn't need your help
I'd be as independent as you please

my servitude is gladly given
for that's what friends are for
there's no shame in being humble
when your doggie asks for more

VII

Over the next months, Rufus began to eat a little more. He continued to hate walks, even though he didn't shiver at being on leash. One behavior we never understood was that, before crossing a driveway, he'd stop, sit, and refuse to move. It took almost three months for him to give that up. Yes, he would walk on leash, but clearly preferred to be off leash. That seemed to work out fine. Without training, he'd walk near us, listen to my commands of "Rufus, wait," or "Come, Rufus."

Carol wrote to Jeanine asking if we could either talk to Rufus' former people or at least learn a little about his background, hoping that knowing more about him would help us better understand and care for him. Jeanine emailed back that his former owners didn't want to have any contact with us. However, she did share as much as she knew of his past.

This is what little we learned:

- We were the third family he had lived with.
- His first family, for reasons Jeanine didn't know, gave him up to the East Valley Pet Shelter. He was about a year or so old.
- He was two days away from being euthanized when Bichons and Buddies rescued him.

- He was adopted by his second family some months after being rescued; a young married couple who wanted a cute, cuddly dog.

- The second family kept him in the yard most of the time. It seems he didn't spend much time in the house or being loved. Rufus is definitely cute, but not so much cuddly.

- The second couple gave him back to Jeanine after a year and a half, telling her they were getting a divorce and neither of them wanted Rufus. Divorce is hard on everyone in the family.

- Bichons and Buddies determined that Rufus was depressed; he would barely eat and didn't show well to potential adopters. They had become resigned to the fact he would probably live with them for a long while and that he'd die young from his depression.

- They were shocked, pleasantly so, when they saw how he behaved with us.

Carol was right; Rufus needed us. He had chosen us to save him. In this life, when you have a chance like that, take it. Sometimes when you're given a choice, you decide based upon what you need. Sometimes you're asked to decide based upon what others need. The more often you make the choice to consider others over yourself, to put another being's needs before your own, the more you realize that it's what you need as well. It's called *compassion*.

VIII

Thanksgiving was just a few days after Rufus joined our family. Our family tradition has me cooking the feast for our daughter her husband, Carol's brother, and our two grandkids. Rufus was excellent. He was friendly with everyone, gave each a chance to pamper him, and didn't beg at the table. He did manage to score a fair share of turkey, however. He loved the mashed potatoes but shunned the dressing. The pumpkin pie went over well with him and everyone else. After that rousing social success, we decided that it was a good idea for Rufus to have a vet visit. We hoped we might learn a little bit more about him, perhaps settle on his age. We figured, taking into account what we knew about his past experiences, he had to be about five years old.

Bichons & Buddies made an appointment with one of the vets who works with them. It was a good visit; no fuss and no apparent health problems. We did indeed learn some new things about Rufus. Though the vet thought Rufus might be as old as seven, we doubted it. She also thought Rufus had the beginnings of an arthritic leg, that he might be limping a bit. Otherwise, she considered him to be a healthy dog. As it turned out, Rufus didn't have any leg problems, at least then, and the funny hop in his step was just one of his special traits.

We introduced Rufus to our neighbors and their children. As he is wherever he goes, Rufus was a big hit. He took a special liking to a three- year-old girl, Ingy, who happens to be my favorite little neighbor, and kept moving over to stand closer to her. All the kids loved him, petted him, gave him treats. He was gentle, sweet, uncomplaining, and a great doggie citizen.

As his personality emerged, his depression lifting, Rufus revealed himself as something of a clown. He loves to burrow in pillows, dive under the covers, and act silly with his toys—he's especially fond of soft and squeaky ones. He's making friends at the dog park more easily. He made two new friends quickly, a rescue Bichon, Simon, who so much looks like him that it's like watching a dog play with his own image. The second buddy was a little yappy chihuahua, with whom he ran around and performed his first play bow. Though, in general, Rufus prefers dogs his own size, he became pals with our friend Lisa's big guy.

Lisa with her rescue pal Seymour, a hundred-plus pound Newfoundland mix, one of Rufus's friends.

THE BARON

After the first month with Rufus, given the way he behaved on Thanksgiving, the way he changed every day to a happier, less depressed dog, the way we—Carol and I—were learning more about him and liking everything we discovered, we knew we had made the right choice.

Carol continued to visit the Bichon & Buddies website, just to look at cute dogs. I saw that Rufus had yet to be taken off the page of dogs available for adoption. I called Bichon & Buddies told them to take Rufus off the site. I let them know that Rufus had found his permanent home with us. We loved this mutt. We believed the feeling was mutual. He greets us with wagging tale and smiles when we come home. He sits by me most of the day while I work away at the computer. He loves to see Carol arrive home from her work. His tail is now constantly resting happily on his back, not down between his legs. Both he and I are learning the best ways to communicate with one another. I've been leaving the front door open and allowing him his choice about when he needs to visit the park. It works well. He goes to the gate and waits for me, I clip him into his new harness, and now he happily walks beside me. At the dog park, whenever he's threatened by a bigger dog, he doesn't cower. He runs to me, sits down beside me. At first, I wasn't sure whether he was asking me to protect him, or if he was standing guard to protect me. It didn't matter. The bond was all that counted. Rufus was bringing his pack together.

We bought him his new tag over the next weekend, proclaiming that he is our companion and loudly announcing his name. I think he appreciated the gesture.

Rufus taught me another important lesson: Put expectations aside; accept and appreciate what's given to you. Rufus was not the dog I pictured when I fantasized about having a canine companion. He's not the standard poodle or the long blond-haired Saluki I always saw sitting next to me while I drove around in my little sports car, his head sticking up proudly, ears blowing in the wind. He's not the energetic, ball-chasing buddy I thought dogs were supposed to be. No. He's Rufus, a gentle, loving soul who needed us as much as we needed him to take away some of the pain from losing Catcher and Pandora. He's his own dog and he's a delight. He's better than my fantasy dog because he's *our* dog. And though I'm still a cat person in my heart, Rufus has burrowed into it, found room beside those felines, became number one. He even let those cats be part of our pack.

I'm no William Wegman, but I try. Here's one of my artsy shots of Rufus.

IX

It took nearly six months before Rufus was really comfortable and begin to show all aspects of his personality. It took a year before he fully came into his own. He became less fearful, more willing to trust us. As I suppose all dogs do, he often chose his behavior in relation to the person he was with. He trained me to feed him from the table, a trick Carol really didn't appreciate. I'm reminded of my duty with a shove of his nose against my leg. I respond as certainly as did Pavlov's animals. He gives me little barks of impatience when I ignore him. He'll do neither to Carol. He goes to Carol first for his scratchies. He likes her a little better than me for that. But until recently, he has always chosen to lie near or under my desk during the day. I believe it's because I work mostly from the house, so he sees me all day long, while Carol works at a production office or on set.

Speaking of being on set, The Baron is invited to be on every one of my sets when I'm working on a show. He's extremely polite, never barks, has never screwed up a shot. He's friendly with everyone. He's a perfect movie dog. If I were a better trainer—more precisely, a trainer at all—with his good looks and fine demeanor, "he coulda been a contender," starring in his own commercials. Of course, I'm prejudiced. But he agrees. He told me, as we sat and watched The

Westminster Dog Show, that he wasn't impressed by these dogs. He felt he had more charisma than any of them.

The Baron Comments on the National Dog Show

Head resting on his red pillow
one eye   open
he watches
a parade of perfect dogs

the Baron is not impressed

even the regal poodle
leaves him quite unmoved
while the lumbering Clumber
buys only his disdain

a little interest peaks
when a bubbly bichon beauty
fluffs her way across the ring

remembering old friends, I suspect

Pedigree he sniffs
a title that holds nothing
against my Baron-ness

his lineage longer than any leash

THE BARON

Look at the way they prance
he comments in his ruffing way
all commoners for certain
surely when it's royalty
in your blood you must remain aloof
dignity in your every move

As Best of Show is chosen
he turns away and chuffs
unwilling to give them due

Later, he lifts his leg
against his favorite spot
dogness in his very bones

produces a stream worthy
of the best of breed

X

Over the ten years we've been together, Rufus, aka The Baron Von Pfeffernusse, and I have grown even closer. He's taught me as much of his language as I could learn. He's come to terms with my peculiarities, accepting me as I am, as dogs always do. He's learned to trust Carol implicitly. He's our perfect dog. He's a good traveler, usually asleep, spread out on the floor under the dash on the passenger side, making whoever isn't driving a little less comfortable than they might otherwise be. But who would deny him that space? Not us. We've learned to live with the inconveniences such as spending more money for a hotel that allows dogs. So he's always a part of our going-away plans. Packing food, treats, litter bags, his bed (won't leave home without it).

We've moved twice since he's been with us. Sold our big house, figuring we could downsize. Though the house was lovely and suited us perfectly when we bought it, we were all getting older—yes, Rufus, too—and our house had three flights of stairs. Plus, he really didn't like the polished wooden floors upon which he too often found himself sliding. The one feature the house lacked—it was a town house—was a backyard. Rufus had to walk two blocks to the park, where he could romp off leash.

THE BARON

We moved to a smaller, one-story place with a nice, fenced front and backyard. Made him happy. Me, too. It meant that all I had to do was open the door in the morning for Rufus to go off, smell the flowers and find the perfect spot for his toilet. As long as we weren't going to get a visit from the mail carrier, a FedEx or UPS delivery, and it wasn't the gardener's day, it was fine to leave the door open for him to roam as he pleased. Anyway, this was Rufus, after all, and spending more than ten minutes or so before coming inside to sleep near me was unthinkable; especially if Carol or I were having breakfast. There's no way he would ever miss the possibility of a people food treat. Okay, I know you're not supposed to feed a dog snacks from the table. But you tell me, if you have looked into the eyes of the companion animal you love, a dog who has learned over the centuries how to use those eyes to entreat, how in the name of Sirius can you refuse? Bad me. I can't.

Three years later, having tired of the Los Angeles traffic, it was now taking me nearly an hour to drive a little over eight miles from our house to a meeting in Hollywood. Given the tension of living in a big city that's still suffering from growing pains, we decided to move to a quieter life. Even though both of us were still working in Los Angeles, we began looking at the 'burbs. We had friends who lived in Palm Springs, but we hadn't considered it an option. Carol doesn't like heat. Me? I'm fine with it. Rufus gave his approval.

We looked everywhere, from the San Fernando Valley, to Santa Barbara, to, well, anyplace within driving distance to Los Angeles. Nothing suited us. Rufus accompanied us on all our trips to find a new home. How could it be otherwise? We needed his approval before we could say "yes" to any house we bought.

Finally, after much coaxing from our friends, we decided to look in the Coachella Valley; that's Palm Springs, Cathedral City, Rancho Mirage, Palm Desert, Indian Wells, La Quinta and Indio. For our first weekend search, we asked our daughter, Denise, who lives with her husband in San Jose, to join us. We value her opinion. We toured about ten places. Many were, to our surprise, lovely homes. And for the first time, I saw the beauty of the desert and the allure of Palm Springs. The air is good. The surrounding mountains, lovely. People were friendly.

The second weekend, just Carol, Rufus and I, visited a bunch more potential home. One place, a smaller condominium community, featured five ponds replete with ducks, a stream running through the property. This delightful mixture of desert landscape, palm trees and seasonal flowers really attracted us. And Rufus.

One of our ponds.

The Baron's view from his patio.

Mama duck and ducklings. Rufus never chases the ducks. He accepts them.

The Baron strolled the grounds happily, peeing on rocks and plants alike, acting very much like the Lord of the Manor, which he truly is. He sniffed toward the ducks; they were the first he'd ever seen, but he didn't bark at them or give them chase. The ducks watched him warily but didn't waddle or fly away.

The people and the property—and the ducks—were dog-friendly. Several places were for sale. At first, I wanted an upstairs condo, so no one could dance upon my head. Carol, wiser is so many ways, pointed out that one of the reasons we sold our big house was the stairs, so we looked only at first-floor homes. We found one, a corner house with additional windows, which meant more light, that we liked. The living room had a big sliding door that opened onto a nice patio and a huge green space. Clearly, potential Rufus territory. After marking the trees and shrubs carefully, and checking out the p-mail, Rufus walked into the condo, walked around the place, carefully sniffed all the spots worth sniffing, went into the tiled guest bathroom, laid down, and went to sleep. We took this as an approval and made an offer on the property.

We spent weekends there for several months before deciding to move permanently from Los Angeles to the desert. August 1, 2017, we became full-time residents of Palm Springs. Rufus went from being a confirmed city dog to becoming a suburban Baron. He demanded ownership of the guest bathroom and asked us to put his bed there. It's his den. He has complete ownership of it. Guests must ask his permission to use the facilities, which he mostly grants. That's another lesson: Rufus taught me adaptability. He's the master of what the host of one of our guilty pleasures, the TV show *Project Runway*, had as his catch phrase: "Make it work." That's what he does. Give him a new circumstance. Give him a conundrum. He doesn't turn away in frustration. He doesn't say, "I quit." What he does is find a way to make it work. Taking his lead, I learned to adapt the way he does. I try to make it work, not fight the given; learn to live with what has been offered me. Nowhere is this more critical, or more difficult, than facing the facts of aging. Rufus is now fifteen. Rufus has lost much of his sight. He has an arthritic left front leg and a weakened rear leg. Imagining what lies before us as The Baron gets older has been hell on Carol and me.

Allen Plone

This is The Baron's sofa. He has first dibs on it.

The Baron Dreams

short sharp barks signal
the Baron's dreams
of younger times

never one to chase a cat
no squirrel suffers
at his snarl

he dreams of protecting
his deep voice
good at warning

keeping his pack safe
from ravaging postmen
FedEx intruders

fearing the Baron's wrath
they run to the safety
of their idling trucks

in his dream
reflecting the truth
of his very being

he is the brave friend
still young vital
content to know
he brought a special love
given only the most worthy

these moments are ours
my Baron
let's cherish them together

Rufus loves living in the desert. He's discovered several new animals he hadn't met before. We have wonderful little lizards scampering all over. Rufus likes to watch them. He followed a roadrunner, keeping distance between him and it so as not to scare the bird, trying to figure out how a dinosaur came to be here with us. Really! He just walked about five or six feet behind the bird until it came to a wall and flew over it. He likes watching the ducks come over to be fed. This isn't allowed in our community, but much like Rufus when he asks for a treat or a belly rub, I have no ability to say "no" to most creatures. Except humans. I can be very judgmental when it comes to many human behaviors. That doesn't include Carol or our daughter. I have trouble saying "no" to any of those three.

Rufus sniffed his first frog, much to the annoyance of the frog. There's a black cat that sometimes comes slinking by at night. Rufus waves hello, then completely ignores her.

He has long conversations with the many ravens who come to eat the bits of apple and seeds I put out for them. Ravens are among my favorite beings. I believe in their magic.

Two frequent visitors.

When I'm not at my computer, Rufus and I often sit outside; he asleep, I try to appreciate a quieter life. Rufus reminds me, another of his many lessons, that it isn't having things that counts. "Sure," he says, "I love my bed. And treats. But what's better is seeing smiles. Feeling love. Being the best friend I can. Being with people, and dogs, you love." For Rufus, it's the richness of being a part of the Universe. To accept the impermanence of all things. Trees lose their leaves; plants, their flowers. All things change. All things end. Even the time with your best friend. He teaches me, every day, how to let things just be. He lets me know that I can't, and never did, own him. His wisdom, how he accepts and adapts, has shown me how much more precious it is to know that, even if for a moment, someone, some living being, chooses to share space and time with you.

When he looks up at me, briefly interrupting his nap, I can see in his now cloudy eyes that he has made a choice to love. As with young children, it comes naturally to him. He reminds me, in his gentle voice, "You have to be taught to hate."

It's his choice to be with me. And be with me totally. If it isn't forever, as nothing is, it's for as long as it needs to be.

XI

Just about a year and a half ago, Rufus started limping badly. He lost weight, seemed uncomfortable—certainly not himself. He developed a deep chest-rattling, honking cough. Carol and I made an appointment with his vet. The vet drew blood for testing. He listened to his heart and called for a series of X-rays.

Dr. Kunz carried him back into the lab and procedures area. We waited in the examining room. He was back there for thirty minutes or so. When he returned, carrying Rufus, Dr. Kunz had the kind of look that is usually the precursor to bad news. "Rufus," said the doctor, "isn't a young guy anymore." We agreed. "He has a heart murmur. Heart problems can cause the cough he has. But I think it's something else. Rufus has a collapsed trachea. He isn't breathing well. That's what's causing the cough." The trachea is the tube that carries oxygen from the nose and mouth to the lungs. All air-breathing animals and humans have one. A collapsing trachea isn't a rare malady among dogs. It can be life-threatening, depending upon how the disease progresses. If the muscles that hold the trachea rigid get too bad, unable to support the tube at all, the dog suffocates and dies. Some dogs (and humans) live a long time with a partially collapsed trachea.

"How serious is it?" I asked.

"With his heart disease, a slightly enlarged liver, his age . . ." I braced for the worst. Carol grabbed my hand. "It's serious."

"How long can he live?" I could hardly get the question out.

"I'd say two, maybe three months."

It isn't as if we hadn't anticipated this. We knew that one day we would lose Rufus. But knowing, anticipating, isn't the thing itself. We cried in the office. We cried driving home. We cried at home. Stoic Rufus just took it all in, sighed, went to his den to take a long nap.

Over the years, there was little I denied Rufus. He wanted treats, he got treats. He wanted his belly rubbed, I plopped onto the floor and rubbed his belly. Now, I resolved, I would really spoil him.

As I mentioned, Rufus, The Baron personified, has always been a fussy eater, especially for a dog. When he first came to live with us, we tried every brand of food, both dry and wet. He turned away from all of them. Yes, we figured, this was part of his depression. And it was. But only a little part. Upon a recommendation from the manager of Centinela Pet Feed, we tried a New Zealand brand called Ziwi Peaks. It's an air-dried food. Rufus took to it with gusto. He especially liked the Mackerel and Lamb combo. It didn't matter, of course, that it's one of the most expensive brands you can purchase.

Rufus has two treats he loves best: fresh-cooked turkey and fresh-cooked tri-tip beef. If he has only a few months to live, I reasoned, he was going to go out in style. I changed his diet to fresh-cooked turkey. Along with rice, which he loves, too, and an occasional taste of canned pumpkin. I mix in a little of the Ziwi Peak to assure that he received the vitamins he needs.

In my sadness, Rufus became one of those over-indulged dogs you might find in a Manhattan Penthouse, sitting upon a velvet cushion wearing a real diamond tiara. Each day Carol and I waited anxiously for his dying, hoping that this day wasn't the one.

A month after his death sentence was pronounced, Rufus was looking and acting better. He started gaining weight, held his tail up over his back again. In general, seemed happier.

Days went by. Weeks. Months. Six months after his vet visit, Rufus was doing more than surviving; he was thriving. He told me, by subtle rejections of his food, that he'd like to go back to his dry dog food. We acquiesced, worrying that the turkey was what made the change. Rufus was back to his old, wonderful, Baron self. No, we didn't stop our vigil. We thought it might be, but hoped it wasn't, one of those short recoveries that happen just before dying.

Rufus relaxes on his patio, more like his old self, watching the world go by.

XII

It's been a year and a half since Dr. Kunz's bleak prognosis. Four months since his pneumonia Rufus's cough hasn't gotten better. Nor has it gotten worse. He's taking longer walks again. His spirit is great. Carol and I still harbor the fear of his dying. Sometimes I wake up at night, go to him in his den, on his bed, to make sure he's breathing.

No, Rufus aka The Baron, didn't teach me how to love. Carol did that. And our daughter. But he did teach me, in his own way and in his own voice, how to love better. He's taught me how to listen to how others speak, not to demand they use only the language I know but to learn theirs. I still sometimes sit, watch him and cry. I'm still preparing for the imminent and inevitable time when he leaves us. I'm determined to enjoy every moment he and I have left together. Sometimes I get lost in the sadness. I tend toward melancholy and moodiness. I'm told it's a writer thing. To me, it's an Allen thing, born from believing that all those I love will someday leave me. I'm working on letting that go, hoping it's one last lesson Rufus teaches me. The sadness aside, I recognize that I have lived a blessed and wonderful life. Carol and I have been together since we met in college. And we're the lucky ones whose love has grown, as we have, over the years. We are constantly happy together. We bring each other joy. I have a wonderful daughter, still in my life despite having a successful life of her own. She, too, is a blessing for which I am forever grateful. I've worked doing only the things I've loved. How lucky is that? And I've been surrounded by companion animals that were the very best friends one could have—two of which stand out as very special to me: Pandy, my familiar, and, of course, Rufus.

I have human friends, many from our college days, whom I love and who love me. I'm thankful for all these blessings. The best man at our wedding, Lee, and Steve and Janet are all one could hope for in friends. They've stood by me even as I have, too often, retreated into my little triad and don't call or see them as much as I should and would really like to.

Now, when I think of The Baron dying, my sadness is tempered by a deep-felt knowledge about our relationship. Rufus's physical presence will leave me. The paw print he placed on my heart the very first day we met, that will never leave.

Poems & Final Thoughts

Over the years, I've written a series of poems about The Baron. You found some of them while reading this book. Since his diagnosis and mistaken death sentence, I've written more; many about both our relationship and his dying. Here are a few.

The first picture I ever took of Rufus. He had become our companion only a few hours prior. He's burrowed under the covers of our bed.

The Baron Looks into the Mirror

does he ask
is that me
worry over
turning hair
the old in his eyes
does he see
what I see
upon reflection
the pup he was
the murmured heart
broken twice
repaired stitched
still beating strong

look back upon himself
judging the moment
in which he always lives
still willing to love
dogness in its grace

sitting near
the one he's chosen
for his own reasons
to be rewarded
with his belly

does he see another like him
an image
of the real Baron
knowing for certain
there can only be
only one

The Baron Grows Older

his cough shakes me
a slower Baron still
unwilling to give up
the royalty of his birth

determined to make the best
it's his way of these pained days
as he begins to fade
leaving a Cheshire smile

no less the young hunter
nose to the ground learning
what the flowers have to tell
which way to stroll today

this unexpected friend
who chose to be loved
despite the disappointments
bestowed in his puppiness

he refuses to feel
like we who fail
to recognize the lined face
in the mirror as ours

can't see the age we were
when our callow selves
had so much to learn
so much before us

he is wiser
knowing it's not length
but quality that defines
the fulfilled life

my Baron
his leg shaking
walks slowly toward his desk
to lie in his bed beneath
choosing as ever to be close

Sonnet for the Slipping Baron

three legs or four for him
there really is no difference
it's truly just a matter of a limb
The Baron travels well   before & since

though his sight is slight
he keeps his Baron's grace
he's not lost the teeth that bite
easily embraces his slower pace

I've lived a strong and happy life
he whispers when he sees me grieve
felt your love   kept me safe from living's strife
but as must   be it's time for me to leave

I told him, never was there a truer braver friend
hand in paw we'll march together towards the end

The Baron Ponders How to Say Goodbye

there's no simple way
says the Baron
knowing all is impermanent
to prepare for saying goodbye

talk all you want
about a life well-lived
keeping alive in memory

there's no substitute
for someone you love
rubbing your belly

is there a kinder way
he wonders
creep away and hide
letting life leave blindly

let sleep go on to ever
but what, when he wakes
and finds me still

with no chance
to say farewell
though spared the pain
of last breaths

won't even consider
the last vet ride
to a needle's finality

in his arms is best
feeling a warm hand
on my always ready back
soothing away age's pains

our tears a stream
washing us
a last time parting

The Baron & the Night Sky

a star falls
near the Baron's nose
waking him

not unfamiliar
with a bit of heaven
he reaches out

nips its nearest point
draws the light closer
into his mouth

where it glows
bright as a sun
from beneath his smile

tossing his head
he launches it skyward
back to the night

where it burns
brighter than ever

THE BARON

Rufus, aka The Baron Von Pfeffernusse

How the World is Changed

the monk and his student
walk together
Guru sighed the student
I worry
I'll never have wisdom enough
to change the world

the Guru stopped
bent down
took a small stone from the path
turned it over in his hand
knelt
placed it back upon the path

See? said the wise one
The world has been changed

The world can be changed by the smallest of actions as long as the action is pure. And even the smallest of actions is pure so long as it's free of anger and fear.

EPILOGUE

Meditation on the beginning of the day.

I'm constantly awed by the nature of creativity; cherish the unknowable depths from which our art arises. For all the suffering and angst the life of an artist often entails, it's a privilege to be a spokesperson for the ineffable and transcendent. I hold no regrets for any part of my life. I lived it as best I knew how. The missteps are as much a part of the journey as the triumphs. I try to take solace in my attempt to always be the best, do the best, create the best I can.

My goal is to live a compassionate and loving life, respectful of all living beings, understanding that we are all one. As I think back to my childhood, those days of formation and transformation are like swimming in a murky sea, a morass of feelings, emotions and puzzles we're not yet able to understand, give voice to—let alone find comfort in. We wander. Some of us are lucky enough to come upon a truer vision of ourselves amidst the morass of living. My blessing was that I was sent a guide, Carol, though at first, neither of us knew it. She shone like a beacon, her strength and love the light to follow. She gave me the will to find purpose.

Born into Judaism, I love my heritage and its traditions. I discovered Buddha's wisdom along the path. I embrace its tenants, its path to a better life. Buddhist thought is a great comfort to me. I live by intention. I try to find the center of things. In gathering into one's self the self, I find that center that expands to encompass the world and love all the sentient beings therein.

Whether as metaphor or actuality, I've been sent a bevy of spirit animals to guide me. Bourgeois, Kishka, Catcher, Pandy and Rufus. Each has taught me things in their own special way. Each has offered their love and companionship. I honor and cherish each one. Perhaps, Rufus, since he's the last of the line, the best. But it's a close call.

As with all moments, as time unfolds upon itself, we meet old friends again, who are part of the journey. Welcome today. Tomorrow isn't a promise. May you all find peace and joy. May you always receive love in the same measure you give it. May you all find companions to travel with you, sharing their love & compassion as I have found mine.

Allen Plone
Cathedral City, California, 2020

1970 - 1977

1978 - 1991

2010 - 2021

1992 - 2007

1992 - 2009

POSTSCRIPT

As I'm writing this, The Baron is asleep on the floor behind my desk. He's taken to pushing pillows around to build a little nest for himself. Yes, he's still alive, still teaching me the values of acceptance and love. He's now well into his doggy dementia, sometimes not knowing where he's at or where he's going. My friend Peter calls it "muttamentia." He sleeps a whole lot more than he used to. But he has his moments. He'll run around the living room, dance back to his bed, beg for more treats – all doggy things to do. My Lazarus of a best friend. In this time of Covid 19, we're all still under stay-at-home orders, his companionship, love and courage is something for which to be grateful.

POST POSTSCRIPT

Rufus died at 4:51 p.m. on March 17th.

Our beloved pet had been in declining health for the last month or so. He was having difficulty breathing, and he couldn't lie down or sleep. Following the advice of our vet, Dr. Phil Caldwell, on Monday we gave him a calming pill, Trazodone, which allowed him to go to sleep and breathe better.

He slept until the following day, a Tuesday, but when he awoke, he was still having breathing problems and seemed more disoriented. He was wobbly on his back legs and sat down every time he tried to walk. We didn't know if this was the effect of the Trazodone or further deterioration. We gave him another dose, at least to allow him to sleep and be calm.

The criteria for taking your furry companion for his final vet trip is usually, "How's his or her quality of life? Are they in pain?" The answer to the pain question is often, "I can't tell." Most of the time your companion can't express whether they're in pain or not. To the first question, how do you separate your need to hold onto them against what they're experiencing?

Rufus had stopped eating, wouldn't take a treat. He hadn't peed in two days. Carol and I agonized, but ultimately decided it was time to say goodbye.

The next morning, we made an appointment with Dr. Caldwell for later that afternoon. Rufus was groggy, probably from the pills, couldn't walk without stumbling. Most of the day we sat next to him, letting him know how much we loved him, how much he gave to us. That he is, always was, always will be a "good dog."

At one point, Rufus stumbled to the door. I opened it. He managed to get half his body out, then laid down. He wanted to feel the sunshine one last time.

Around 4:30 that afternoon, I lifted him up and carried him to the car. As we left the house, he looked at me, reached up, gave me a kiss, his last one, right on my lips. At the vet's office, we held him as he was injected, sending him on his last journey.

THE BARON

The house feels emptier. I wake up looking for him. His spirit, his love, his friendship, his wisdom pervades our house and still helps make it a home. The feeling may dissipate over time. I hope not. I will likely never get over his loss, as I have never really gotten over the loss of our other companions. But it's okay. No, there's no hole in my heart. Rufus adequately fills it up.

Goodbye sweet dog, Rufus, aka The Baron. May the breadth of your spirit encompass the universe and make it better.

Allen Plone
March 19, 2021
Palm Springs, California

MORE FROM ALLEN PLONE

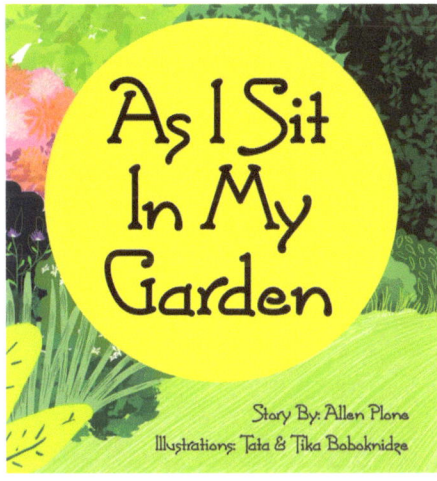

Found wherever great books are sold.